Grades 1-5

TRADITIONAL TALES
to SING & TELL

featuring

Jack & The Beanstalk • Goldilocks & The Three Bears
The Diggity Drummer Of Dawgtown • The Giant Turnip

S0-ENU-674

Reproducible Pages!

Arranged For Orff Instruments & Piano
By Donna Dirksing

Editor: Kris Kropff
Book Design: Patti Jeffers
Music Engraving: Jeanette Dotson
Cover Design: Patrick Doran

© 2007 Heritage Music Press, a division of The Lorenz Corporation, and its licensors. All rights reserved.

Permission to photocopy the student pages in this book is hereby granted to one teacher as part of the purchase price. This permission may only be used to provide copies for this teacher's specific classroom or educational setting. This permission may not be transferred, sold, or given to any additional or subsequent user of this product. Thank you for respecting the copyright laws.

Printed in the United States of America

ISBN: 978-0-89328-596-8

HMP
HERITAGE MUSIC PRESS
A Division of The Lorenz Corporation
Box 802 / Dayton, OH 45401-0802
www.lorenz.com

Foreword

Anyone who is familiar with children knows that kids enjoy listening to stories. But music teachers know that children especially like stories that include songs and music. We know that children enjoy pausing a story in order to reflect using song and movement. We know that children enjoy the predictability of singing a recurring song. But most of all, music teachers know that children enjoy becoming part of the storytelling through music. This participation is the hook that keeps our students asking for more.

Traditional Tales to Sing and Tell is a collection of well-loved children's stories and corresponding songs that are interspersed in each story. Each song includes a simple piano accompaniment and an optional Orff arrangement. All of the Orff arrangements are basic and can be learned in minimal time. These arrangements can also be played by or easily adapted for Boomwhackers®. No matter which accompaniment option you choose, your students will love embellishing the story by singing.

Now have a great time and let the tales begin!

—Donna Dirksing

Contents

Teaching Tips and Extensions	3
The Wide-Mouthed Frog	6
Flies, Flies Reproducible Lyric Sheet	10
Piano Accompaniment	11
Orff Accompaniment	12
"Treats" Reproducible Page (for optional extension)	13
THE GIANT TURNIP	14
The Giant Turnip Reproducible Lyric Sheet	19
Piano Accompaniment	20
Orff Accompaniment	21
Jack and the Beanstalk	22
Jack's Song Reproducible Lyric Sheet	28
The Giant Reproducible Page	29
Piano Accompaniment	30
Orff Accompaniment	31
Goldilocks and the Three Bears	34
Yonder Come Day Reproducible Lyric Sheet	40
Somebody... Reproducible Lyric Sheet	41
Piano Accompaniment	42
Orff Accompaniment	44
The Diggity Drummer of DawgTown	47
Cats Reproducible Lyric Sheet	54
The Dawg Song Reproducible Lyric Sheet	55
Piano Accompaniment	56
Orff Accompaniment	60

Teaching Tips and Extensions

As you begin using *Traditional Tales to Sing and Tell,* think of the many language arts and literacy concepts that you incorporate into your music classroom. Listening to stories is an integral part of the reading process. As they listen, your students strengthen their comprehension skills. They imagine the sequence of events as the plot unfolds and predict coming events and outcomes. The songs in this book can be taught through echo imitation or by reproducing or projecting the lyrics. As your students familiarize themselves with the songs, they will sound out words and also identify short and long vowel sounds, syllables, phrases, and rhyming words. The stories themselves can also be reproduced so that your students can enjoy being the narrators. One thing is for certain: your students will reinforce and strengthen their literacy skills. Make the most of the children's experience by asking them to share this knowledge with you along the way.

Not only do children enjoy listening to stories, they also like to act them out. Your students may enjoy pantomiming movements or acting out events while you read to them. Invite students to take turns narrating. This exploration of pantomime and narration might even give way to a final performance. The students could invite their classroom teacher or the principal. Add some simple props and invite other grade levels or parents to attend the performance.

Your students can also create illustrations to accompany the events in each story. You can assign events or allow the students to illustrate one of their favorite scenes. These illustrations will be fun to display as your class reads and sings the story. Some of the kids might even "donate" their illustrations so that you can use them with future students.

With a trip to your favorite bookstore you will find a myriad of picture books that can complement these tales; just add the songs in the appropriate spots. Continue the cross-curricular extensions by comparing and contrasting similarities and differences between the versions of each tale.

No matter how you use the stories, be sure to have a great time reading them aloud to your students. Kids love hearing a story that is kid-like; be silly at times, and change your vocal inflection. Create different voices for the different characters. Keep the kids on the edges of their seats by adding dramatic pauses, facial expressions and irony in your voice. Surprise them by suddenly becoming softer or louder. Not only will your students be engaged in the story and eager to sing, they will love the experience.

The Wide-Mouthed Frog

Orff Instruments
Soprano and Alto Glockenspiels
Alto and Bass Xylophones

Extension
Brainstorm a list of other tasty treats a wide-mouthed frog might like to eat. The children can draw a picture of their favorite treat and write its name underneath. Create new verses by having the children hold up their picture when it's time to sing *Flies, Flies*. The class then sings the song with that treat in place of "flies". Or, create a larger visual of the song lyrics and have the children tape their treat onto that visual. You could sing them in order or have a student conductor point to the treat the class will sing. (If you choose the latter, be sure to let each student have a chance to be the conductor.)

Pressed for time? A reproducible page with pictures of the treats worms, cake, snacks, and kids is provided on page 13. Copy the picture page and cut it into quarters, giving each child a picture of one of the treats. Each child can write the name of the treat underneath the picture and color, if time allows. These pictures may then be used as outlined above.

THE GIANT TURNIP

Orff Instruments
Soprano and Alto Glockenspiels
Soprano, Alto and Bass Xylophones
Soprano, Alto and Bass Metallophones

Teaching Tips
Use movement to reinforce the steady beat throughout *The Giant Turnip*. Begin by saying "PULL TUG PULL TUG" to the pulse. Then, reach in front of the body, mimicking the motions of grabbing an imaginary vine on the word "PULL" and tugging on the vine on the word "TUG." Continue this motion while singing the song. Prepare the Glockenspiel part by having the students clap or snap the Glockenspiel rhythm while singing the song.

If you choose to use the Orff accompaniment, consider having the Xylophone and Metallophone players continue to speak PULL and TUG to help with the transfer.

Jack and the Beanstalk

Orff Instruments
Soprano and Alto Glockenspiels
Soprano and Alto Xylophones
Soprano and Alto Metallophones
Bass Xylophone
Bass Metallophone
Vibraslap, Woodblock, Tambourine, Drum

Teaching Tips
There are two songs in this story: *Jack's Song* and *The Giant*. *Jack's Song* is sung multiple times and the action verb in the song is changed to match the story. All of the version of *Jack's Song* except "water," which is notated, match the structure of "wait/waiting." The action verb is listed on the story pages, as well as on the reproducible lyric sheet.

Students can perform the action verb to the beat while singing the song in order to prepare the Bass Xylophone part. The Soprano and Alto Xylophone part can be prepared by clapping the rhythm while singing; the Glockenspiel part can be prepared by snapping the rhythm while singing.

A reproducible page of *The Giant* in stick notation is provided on page 29 as a teaching tool.

Goldilocks and the Three Bears

Orff Instruments
Soprano and Alto Glockenspiels
Soprano, Alto and Bass Xylophones
Maracas

Teaching Tips
The song *Yonder Come Day* serves as the introduction and coda for this familiar story. Be sure that students are swinging the melody, as well as the three-eighth-note pattern in the xylophone part. The Orff accompaniment can be prepared by patting the Bass Xylophone part, snapping the Soprano and Alto Xylophone part, and clapping the Glockenspiel part while singing the song.

During the first part of the story, as Goldilocks explores the home of the Three Bears, students will echo Goldilocks's response to each item (e.g. Too hot! Too cold!), and end with "Naughty Goldilocks," before she moves to the next item. (These responses are included in the story.)

The song *Somebody...* is sung in response to the Bears' reaction at finding their home in disarray. The melody is the same, while the lyrics change as they find their pudding, chair and bed, respectively. The Orff accompaniment for this song features a simple broken bordun in the xylophones, so you might consider using it even if your students aren't ready for the Orff parts in *Yonder Come Day*. (One or more parts can always be omitted to make the arrangement more suitable for younger students.)

The Diggity Drummer of DawgTown

Orff Instruments
Soprano, Alto and Bass Xylophones
Shaker
Drum

Teaching Tips
Two songs—*Cats* and *The Dawg Song*—complement this fun story. Both songs have a swing feel and are performed independently before partnering as the Diggity Drummer leads the cats out of town.

To match the swing feel, students should snap on beats 2 and 4 while singing *Cats*. Snaps can be transferred to the shaker whether or not you choose to use the Orff accompaniment.

You may choose to have one student be The Diggity Drummer of DawgTown, or you could assign several students to this song and/or drum part. (Using multiple students will obviously make balance easier, but using a soloist is effective in performance and provides a "teachable moment" regarding the importance of dynamics.)

"Instructions" for the drum part are given in the story. The drummer should begin softly when indicated and continue to play for the reminder of the story, getting louder and softer as directed by the story. The rhythm is given in the story and is also on the reproducible lyric sheet for *The Dawg Song*. Also, this is the same rhythm that the drum plays in the Orff arrangement, with the exception of the last measure.

The Wide-Mouthed Frog

A wide-mouthed frog hopped through the jungle. It was the hottest day of the year and the air conditioner in his pad had stopped working. He wanted to cool off by taking a dip in the jungle swamp.

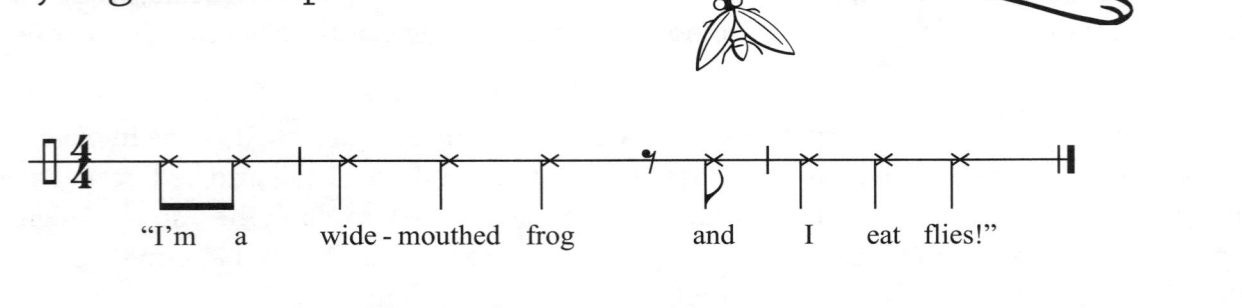

"I'm a wide-mouthed frog and I eat flies!"

He said, and he leaped into the water of the swamp.

♪ Sing *Flies, Flies*

Flies, flies are what I eat. Flies, flies make lunch com-plete. My mouth o-pens wide and I stick my tongue out. I'm a wide-mouthed frog and that's what I'm a-bout.

From *Traditional Tales to Sing and Tell*, by Donna Dirksing. Permission to reproduce is granted for single-classroom use.

The wide-mouthed frog jumped onto a log in the middle of the swamp. He looked around and saw a lizard sunning herself on a rock. He said to her,

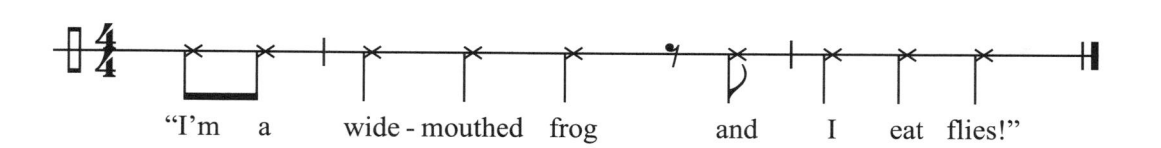

"I'm a wide-mouthed frog and I eat flies!"

🎵 Sing *Flies, Flies*

"Well, I usually eat bugs but I most prefer candy bars. And I beg your pardon, you have disturbed my suntan." The lizard scurried away. So the wide-mouthed frog leaped back into the water. He swam around in the swamp and after awhile he saw a turtle resting in the shallow water. He said to him,

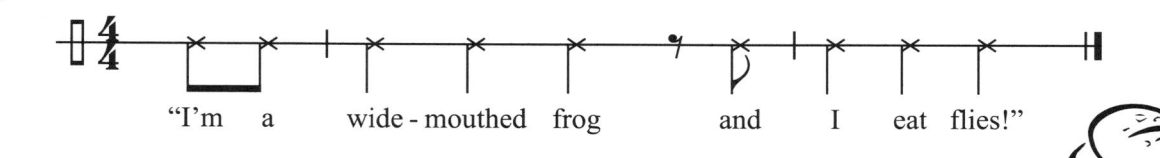

"I'm a wide-mouthed frog and I eat flies!"

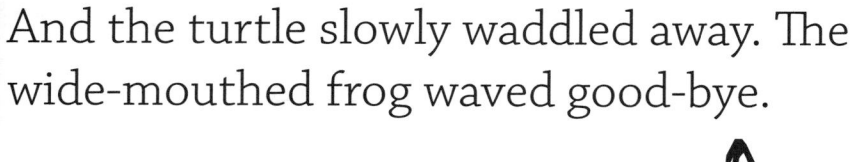

🎵 Sing *Flies, Flies*

"Well, I usually eat seaweed but I most prefer hamburgers. And I beg your pardon, you have disturbed my dream." And the turtle slowly waddled away. The wide-mouthed frog waved good-bye.

From *Traditional Tales to Sing and Tell*, by Donna Dirksing. Permission to reproduce is granted for single-classroom use.

The wide-mouthed frog hopped up to the shore so that he could dry off a bit. He saw a giraffe peeking at him through the trees and he said to her,

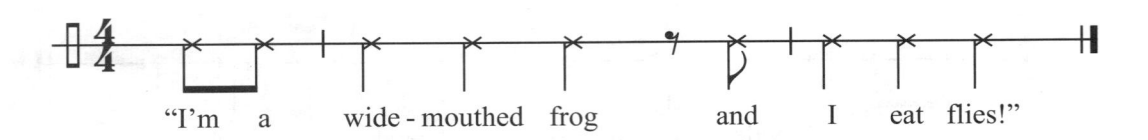

"I'm a wide-mouthed frog and I eat flies!"

🎵 Sing *Flies, Flies*

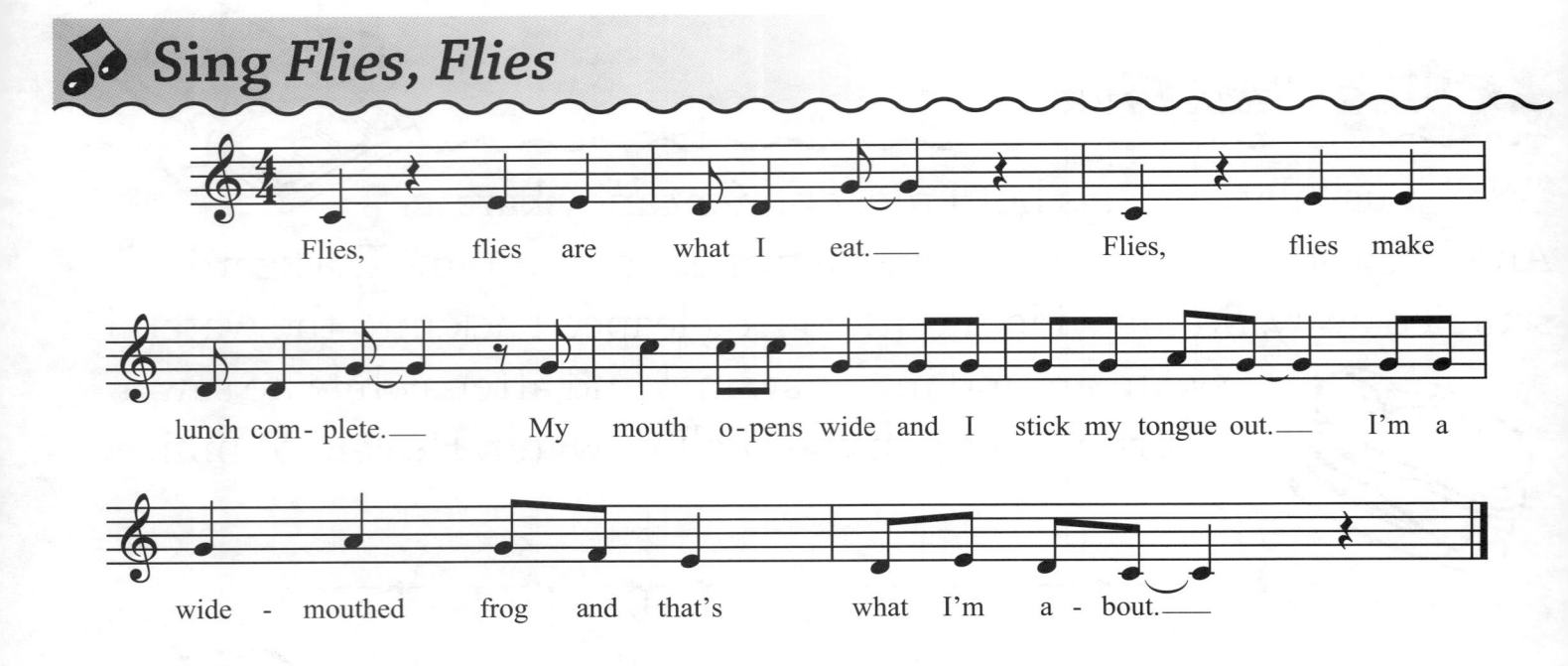

Flies, flies are what I eat. Flies, flies make lunch com-plete. My mouth o-pens wide and I stick my tongue out. I'm a wide-mouthed frog and that's what I'm a-bout.

"Well, I usually eat leaves but I most prefer ice cream. And I beg your pardon, you have disturbed my walk." And the giraffe walked away far into the jungle.

From *Traditional Tales to Sing and Tell*, by Donna Dirksing. Permission to reproduce is granted for single-classroom use.

The wide-mouthed frog saw something moving in the leaves. A snake was slithering down a tree limb. The wide-mouthed frog said to him,

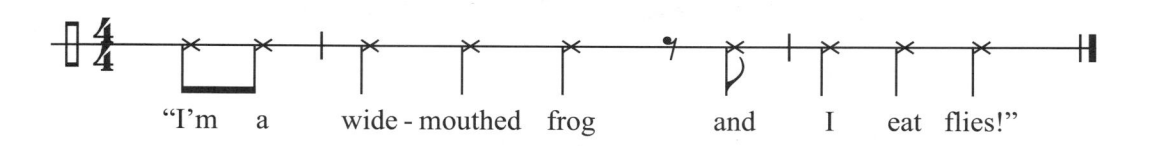

"I'm a wide-mouthed frog and I eat flies!"

🎵 Sing *Flies, Flies*

"Well, I eat lots of things but I most prefer wide-mouthed frogs. And I beg your pardon, but what kind of frog did you say that you were?" said the snake. "Umm...," said the wide-mouthed frog, puckering up his lips as tight as he could. "I am just a plain old frog—one with a very small mouth." And he quickly hopped away back to his home. He definitely needed to fix his air conditioner.

Flies, Flies

Flies, flies are what I eat.

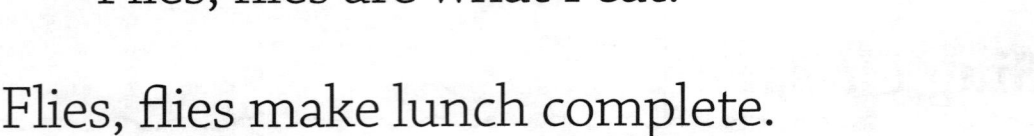

Flies, flies make lunch complete.

My mouth opens wide and I stick my tongue out.

I'm a wide-mouthed frog and that's what I'm about.

From *Traditional Tales to Sing and Tell*, by Donna Dirksing. Permission to reproduce is granted for single-classroom use.

Flies, Flies

Piano

Donna Dirksing

Flies, flies are what I eat. Flies, flies make lunch com-plete. My mouth o-pens wide and I stick my tongue out. I'm a wide-mouthed frog and that's what I'm a-bout.

11

Flies, Flies

Orff Accompaniment   **Donna Dirksing**

Flies, flies are what I eat. Flies, flies make lunch com-plete. My mouth o-pens wide and I stick my tongue out. I'm a wide-mouthed frog and that's what I'm a-bout.

I like to eat!

Yeah!

From *Traditional Tales to Sing and Tell*, by Donna Dirksing. Permission to reproduce is granted for single-classroom use.

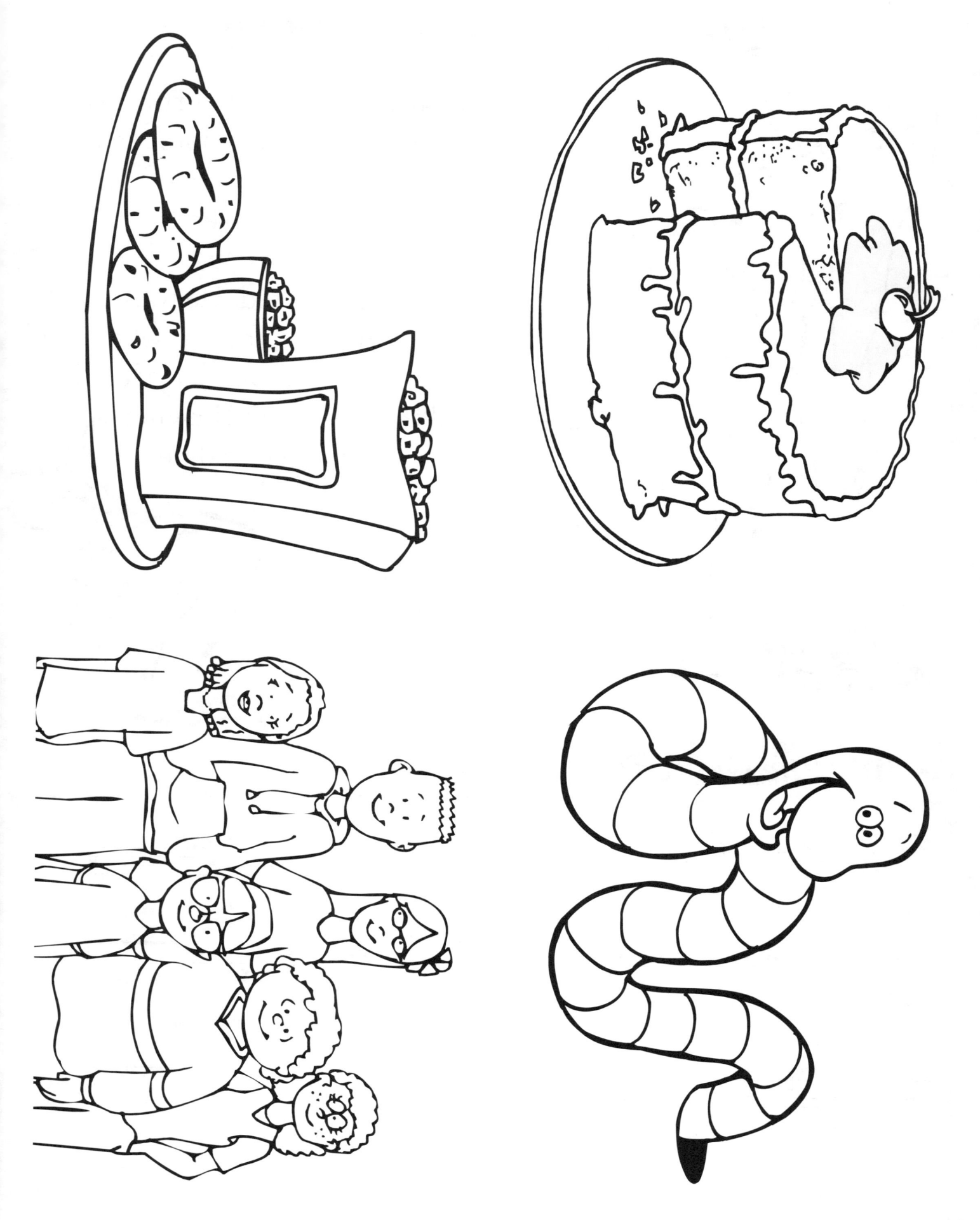

13

THE GIANT TURNIP

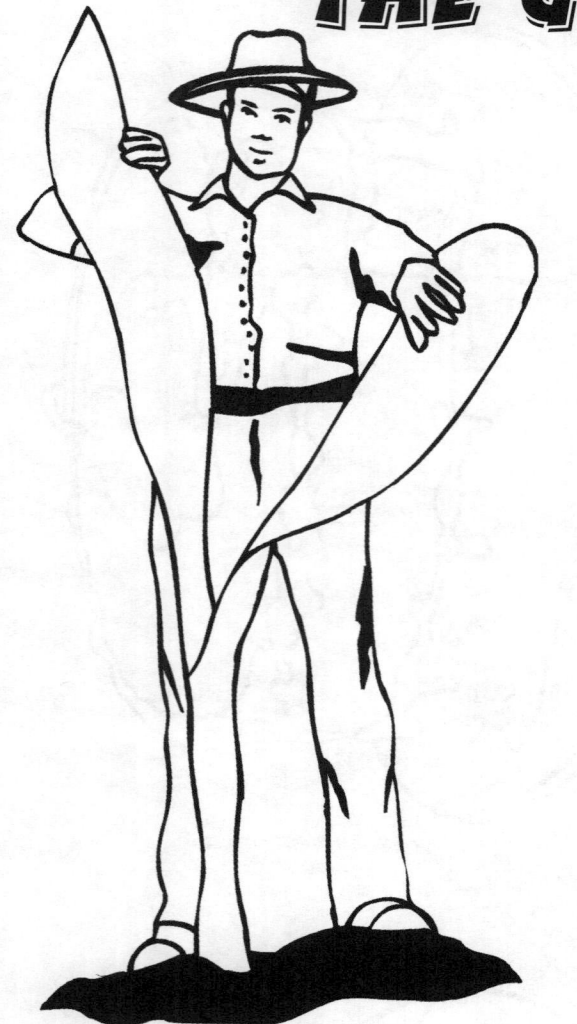

One day a farmer planted a turnip seed. He watered and tended the sprout until finally a turnip began to grow. It grew and grew until it was a giant-sized turnip.

The farmer was so excited. He wanted to take his giant turnip to the fair where he knew it would win first prize. He leaned over to pull the turnip off the vine. He pulled and he tugged and he pulled and he tugged but the turnip would not snap off the vine. "Oh drat!" said the farmer.

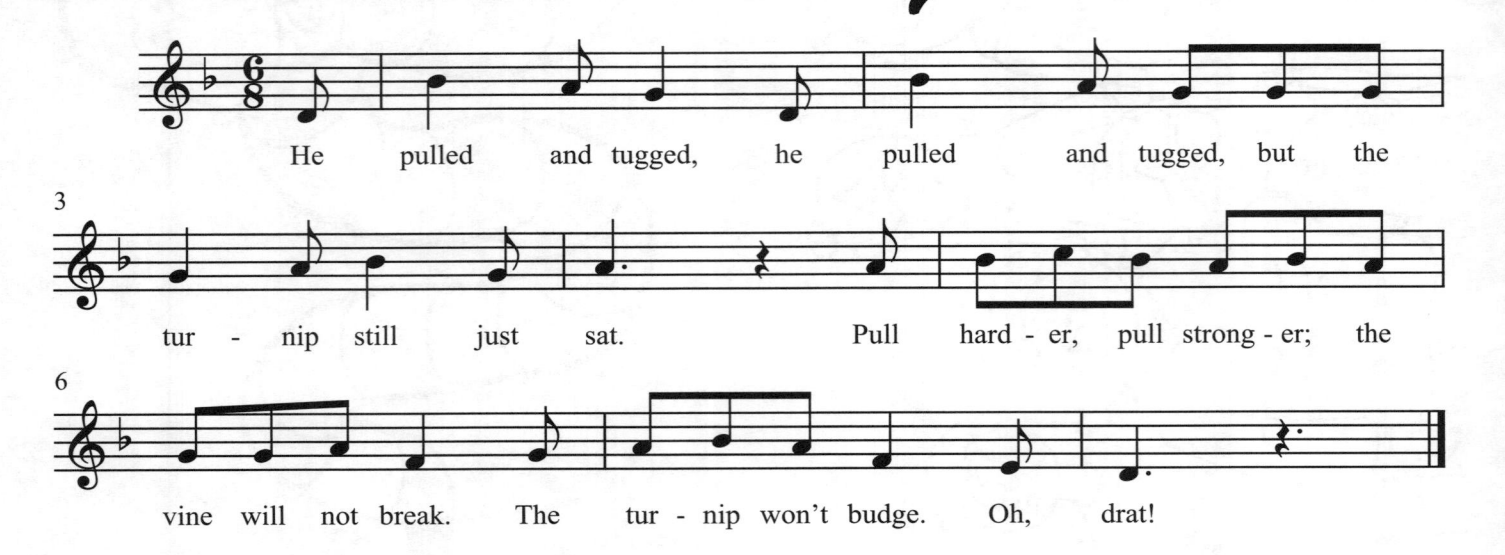

♪♪ Sing *The Giant Turnip*

He pulled and tugged, he pulled and tugged, but the tur-nip still just sat. Pull hard-er, pull strong-er; the vine will not break. The tur-nip won't budge. Oh, drat!

14   From *Traditional Tales to Sing and Tell*, by Donna Dirksing. Permission to reproduce is granted for single-classroom use.

The farmer's wife saw what the farmer was doing. The wife was an excellent cook and she said to the farmer, "You know that I have a way with food. I know that I can get that turnip off the vine." She leaned over to pull the turnip. She pulled and she tugged and she pulled and she tugged but the turnip would not snap off the vine. "Oh drat!" said the farmer's wife.

🎵 Sing *The Giant Turnip*

She pulled and tugged, she pulled and tugged, but the tur-nip still just sat. Pull hard-er, pull strong-er; the vine will not break. The tur-nip won't budge. Oh, drat!

From *Traditional Tales to Sing and Tell*, by Donna Dirksing. Permission to reproduce is granted for single-classroom use.

The farmer's son saw what his mother and father were doing and offered his help. "I am much younger and stronger than both of you. I will get the turnip off the vine." He leaned over to pull the turnip. He pulled and he tugged and he pulled and he tugged but the turnip would not snap off the vine. "Oh drat!" said the farmer's son.

♪ Sing *The Giant Turnip*

He pulled and tugged, he pulled and tugged, but the tur-nip still just sat. Pull hard-er, pull strong-er; the vine will not break. The tur-nip won't budge. Oh, drat!

From *Traditional Tales to Sing and Tell*, by Donna Dirksing. Permission to reproduce is granted for single-classroom use.

The family was not yet defeated. They saw their dog Buster and called for him to come over. "Buster loves to play tug," said the farmer. "He will surely get the turnip off the vine." Buster ran over to pull the turnip. He pulled and he tugged and he pulled and he tugged but the turnip would not snap off the vine. "Oh drat!" said the family.

🎵 Sing *The Giant Turnip*

Now they were frustrated. No one could believe that their giant turnip might not get first prize at the fair. They were almost ready to give up when suddenly a rat appeared. The farmer looked at his son and smirked. The son looked at his mother and sighed. She looked at the men and smiled. "This rat will get our giant turnip off the vine for us."

The rat began to gnaw through the vine. The farmer and his son looked at each other and smiled. The wife pulled the farmer, the farmer pulled his son, and the son pulled the vine. The rat continued to gnaw with all its might. Then...SNAP!

From *Traditional Tales to Sing and Tell*, by Donna Dirksing. Permission to reproduce is granted for single-classroom use.

The vine broke and the turnip flew through the air. The family raced after it. They followed the turnip as it bounced and bounced, and bounced and bounced down the hill. The turnip finally stopped bouncing right at the fair where the judges were sizing up all the turnips. They had never seen such a giant turnip and they quickly awarded it first prize. "We won first prize. Hooray for the rat!" cried the farmer and his family.

♪ Sing *The Giant Turnip* (Final)

They pulled and tugged, they pulled and tugged, but the tur-nip still just sat. When it broke free they were filled with glee. Hoo-ray for the rat!

From *Traditional Tales to Sing and Tell*, by Donna Dirksing. Permission to reproduce is granted for single-classroom use.

THE GIANT TURNIP

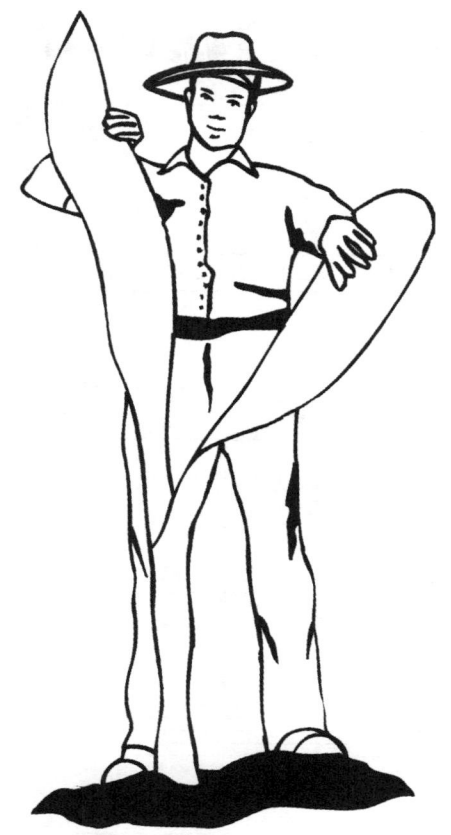

He pulled and tugged,
He pulled and tugged,
But the turnip still just sat.

Pull harder, pull stronger;
The vine will not break.
The turnip won't budge. Oh, drat!

They pulled and tugged,
They pulled and tugged,
But the turnip still just sat.

When it broke free
They were filled with glee.
Hooray for the rat.

From *Traditional Tales to Sing and Tell*, by Donna Dirksing. Permission to reproduce is granted for single-classroom use.

THE GIANT TURNIP

PIANO

DONNA DIRKSING

He/She pulled and tugged, he/she pulled and tugged, but the
(Final) They pulled and tugged, they pulled and tugged, but the

tur-nip still just sat. Pull hard-er, pull strong-er; the
tur-nip still just sat. When it broke free they were

vine will not break. The tur-nip won't budge. Oh, drat!
filled with glee. Hoo-ray for the rat!

THE GIANT TURNIP

ORFF ACCOMPANIMENT — DONNA DIRKSING

He/She pulled and tugged, he/she
(Final) They pulled and tugged, they
pulled and tugged, but the turnip still just sat. Pull harder, pull stronger; the
pulled and tugged, but the turnip still just sat. — When it broke free they were
vine will not break. The turnip won't budge. Oh, drat!
filled with glee. Hooray for the rat!

Pull! Tug! Pull! Tug! Etc.

21

Jack and the Beanstalk

One day a boy named Jack was playing in his Grandma's attic when he noticed a large bag that said *Magic Beans.* Jack picked up the bag and read the label: *Plant these beans and big things will come.*

Jack was so excited about his find that he took the bag, ran downstairs, went outside and quickly dug a hole in the ground. He planted the beans and he waited. He waited and waited but nothing happened.

♪ Sing *Jack's Song*

Wait wait wait wait wait wait wait wait wait wait wait, I say.
Wait-ing wait-ing wait-ing wait-ing all the time a-way.
All I want to do is play. But
wait wait wait wait wait wait wait-ing must be done to-day.

22 From *Traditional Tales to Sing and Tell*, by Donna Dirksing. Permission to reproduce is granted for single-classroom use.

Jack woke up the next morning and went outside to check on the beans. He watered the beans and waited. He watered and watered but nothing happened. "I hope that I didn't find a bum bag of beans," said Jack.

♪ Sing *Jack's Song*

Wa-ter wa-ter wa-ter wa-ter wa-ter I say.

Wa-ter wa-ter wa-ter wa-ter all the time a-way.

All I want to do is play. But

wa-ter wa-ter wa-ter wa-t'ring must be done to-day.

From *Traditional Tales to Sing and Tell*, by Donna Dirksing. Permission to reproduce is granted for single-classroom use.

When a sprout began to peek out of the ground, Jack was so excited. The sprout grew and grew. Soon the sprout had grown clear into the clouds. Jack could hardly believe his eyes!

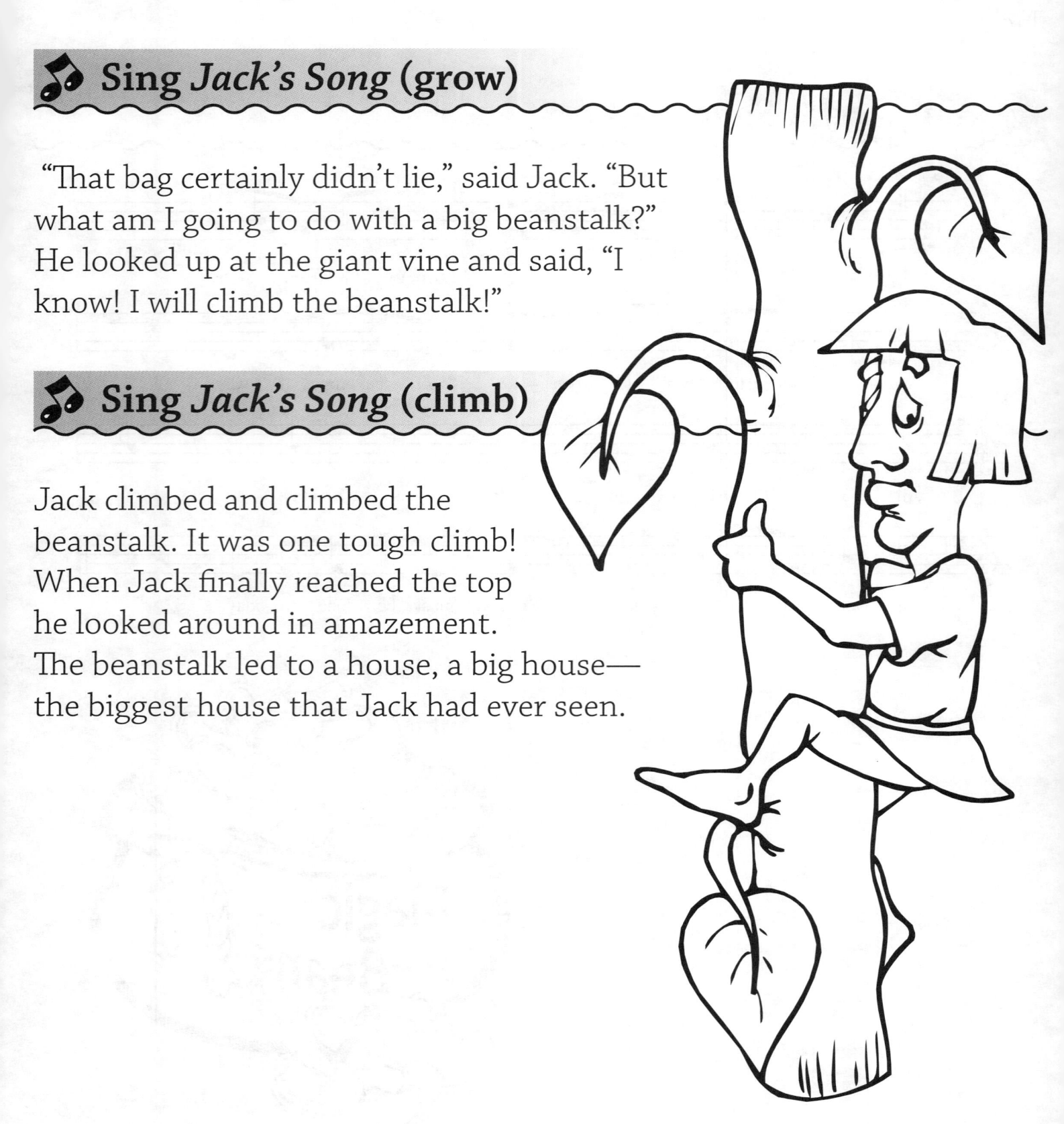

🎵 Sing *Jack's Song* (grow)

"That bag certainly didn't lie," said Jack. "But what am I going to do with a big beanstalk?" He looked up at the giant vine and said, "I know! I will climb the beanstalk!"

🎵 Sing *Jack's Song* (climb)

Jack climbed and climbed the beanstalk. It was one tough climb! When Jack finally reached the top he looked around in amazement. The beanstalk led to a house, a big house—the biggest house that Jack had ever seen.

Jack thought that he smelled cookies and he was pretty hungry from all that climbing. "Maybe someone in the big house has baked cookies. I'm going to sneak in and see."

🎵 Sing *Jack's Song* (sneak)

Jack opened the door to the big house and sneaked around inside. Jack looked around and saw that everything was big—the chairs, the table, the kitchen. He wondered who could live in such a giant place.

Jack walked into the kitchen. Sure enough, there were cookies cooling on a big table. "I'll have just one cookie before I go home," said Jack as he munched on a cookie.

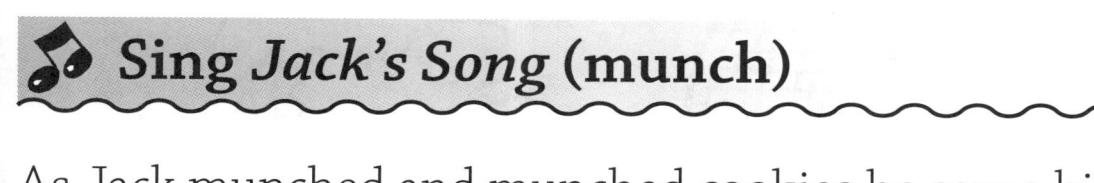

🎵 Sing *Jack's Song* (munch)

As Jack munched and munched cookies he saw a big glass filled with milk. "Some milk would really hit the spot," and Jack took some sips from the big glass of milk.

🎵 Sing *Jack's Song* (sip)

Jack was so busy enjoying his snack that he didn't hear someone open the front door. A big man—a giant man—lived in the house and he had just arrived home from his tennis lesson. He wasn't happy to find Jack eating his cookies.

Speak *The Giant*

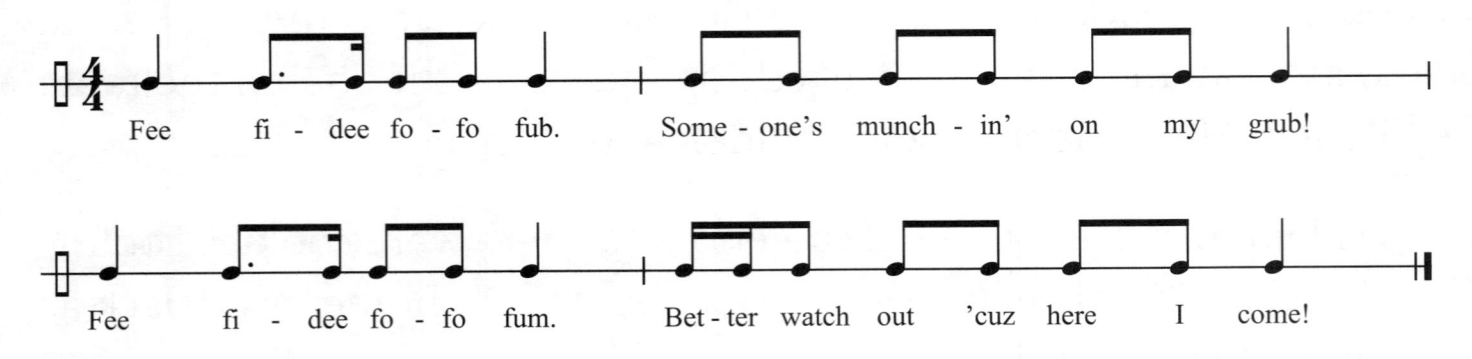

Fee fi - dee fo - fo fub. Some - one's munch - in' on my grub!

Fee fi - dee fo - fo fum. Bet - ter watch out 'cuz here I come!

Jack didn't notice that the giant had come into the kitchen and was looking right at him.

Speak *The Giant*

Jack took one look at the giant and ran back to the beanstalk with all his might. The giant followed after him but Jack was nimble.

♪ Sing *Jack's Song* (run)

Jack climbed down the beanstalk with all his might. The giant was gaining speed but Jack was quick.

🎵 Sing *Jack's Song* (climb)

Jack grabbed an ax and chopped down the beanstalk with all his might. That giant was getting close now. Jack had to hurry!

🎵 Sing *Jack's Song* (chop)

Snap!...went the beanstalk. *"Timber!"* yelled Jack. *Thud!*...landed the giant.

Jack thought that his troubles were over. But after a few moments Jack became very worried about the giant. He could be hurt or in pain. Jack ran inside and called a flat-bed tow truck. The nice truckers took the giant to the hospital.

The next day Jack rode his bike to the hospital to visit the giant. The giant had a broken leg and a bump on his head but was in otherwise good spirits. He and Jack enjoyed cookies and milk and talked all afternoon. They became best friends.

From *Traditional Tales to Sing and Tell*, by Donna Dirksing. Permission to reproduce is granted for single-classroom use.

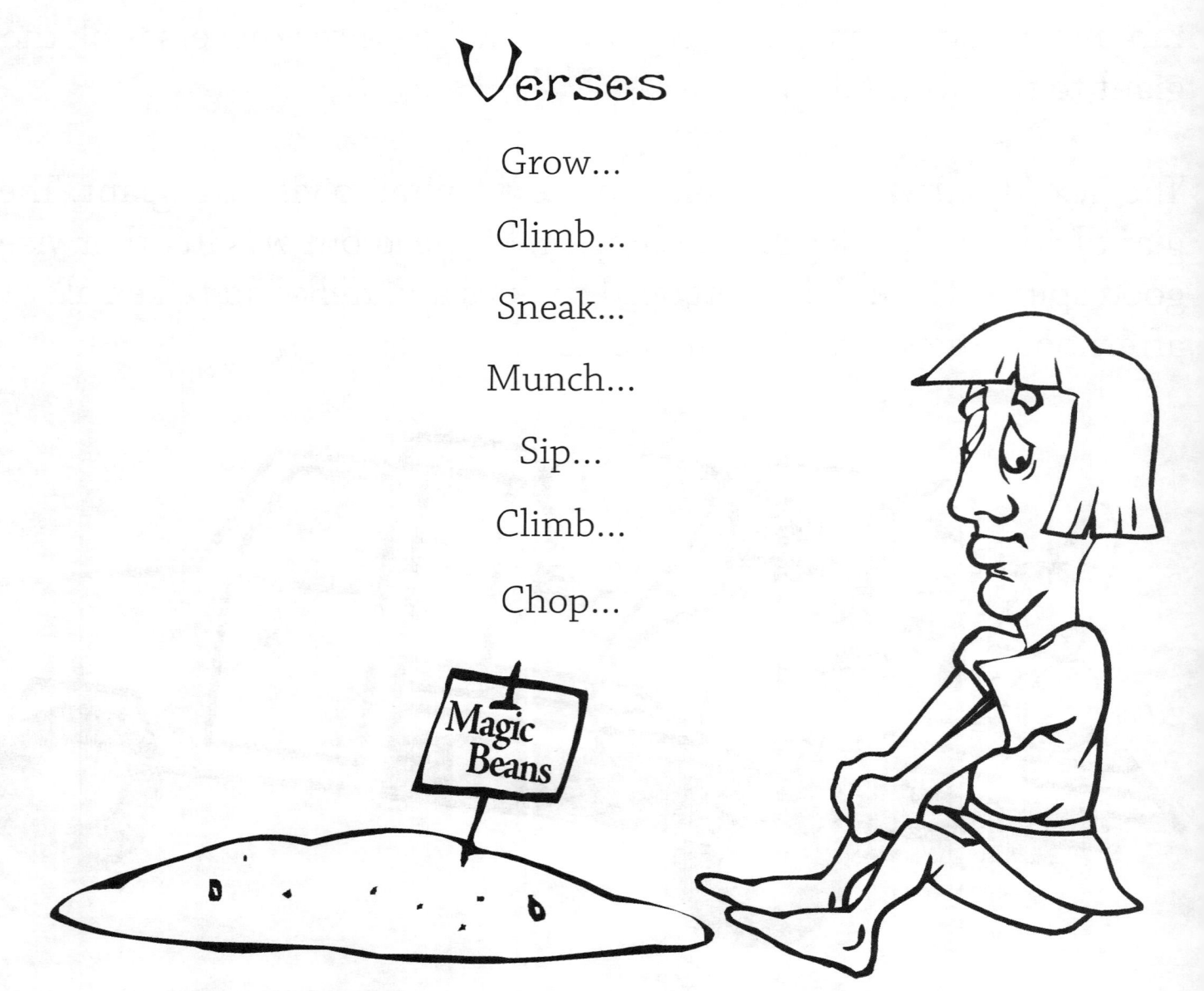

Jack's Song

Wait wait wait wait wait wait wait wait
Wait wait wait, I say
Waiting waiting waiting waiting
Wait the time away.

All I want to
do is play.
But wait wait wait wait wait wait waiting
Must be done today.

Verses

Grow...

Climb...

Sneak...

Munch...

Sip...

Climb...

Chop...

From *Traditional Tales to Sing and Tell*, by Donna Dirksing. Permission to reproduce is granted for single-classroom use.

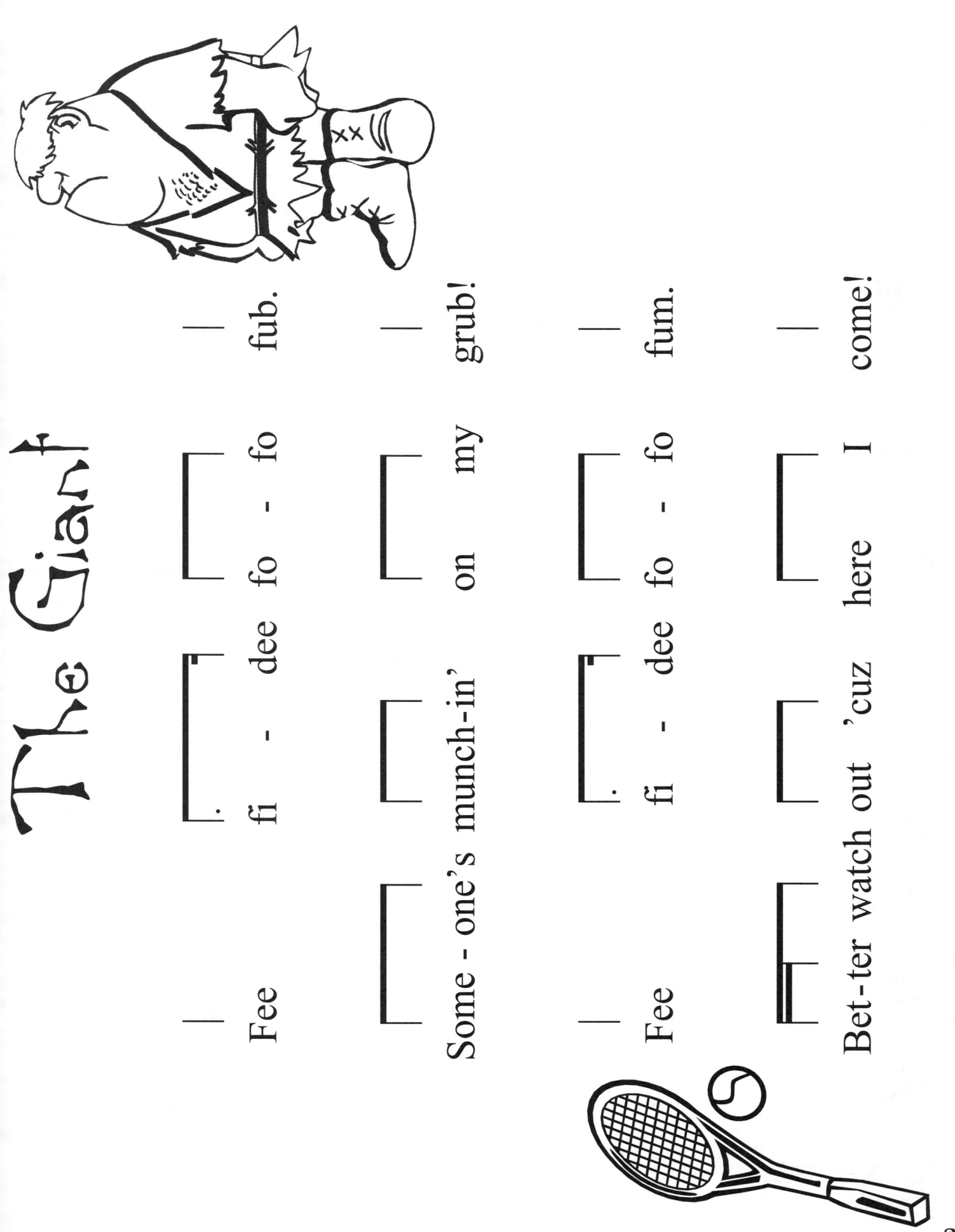

The Giant

Fee fi - dee fo - fo — fub.

Some - one's munch-in' on my grub!

Fee fi - dee fo - fo — fum.

Bet - ter watch out 'cuz here I come!

From *Traditional Tales to Sing and Tell*, by Donna Dirksing. Permission to reproduce is granted for single-classroom use.

Jack's Song

Piano

Donna Dirksing

Wait wait wait wait wait wait wait wait wait wait wait, I say.

Wait-ing wait-ing wait-ing wait-ing all the time a-way.

All I want to do is play. But

wait wait wait wait wait wait wait-ing must be done to-day.

Jack's Song

Orff Accompaniment — Donna Dirksing

Wait wait wait wait wait wait wait wait wait wait wait, I say.

Wait-ing wait-ing wait-ing wait-ing all the time a-way.

32

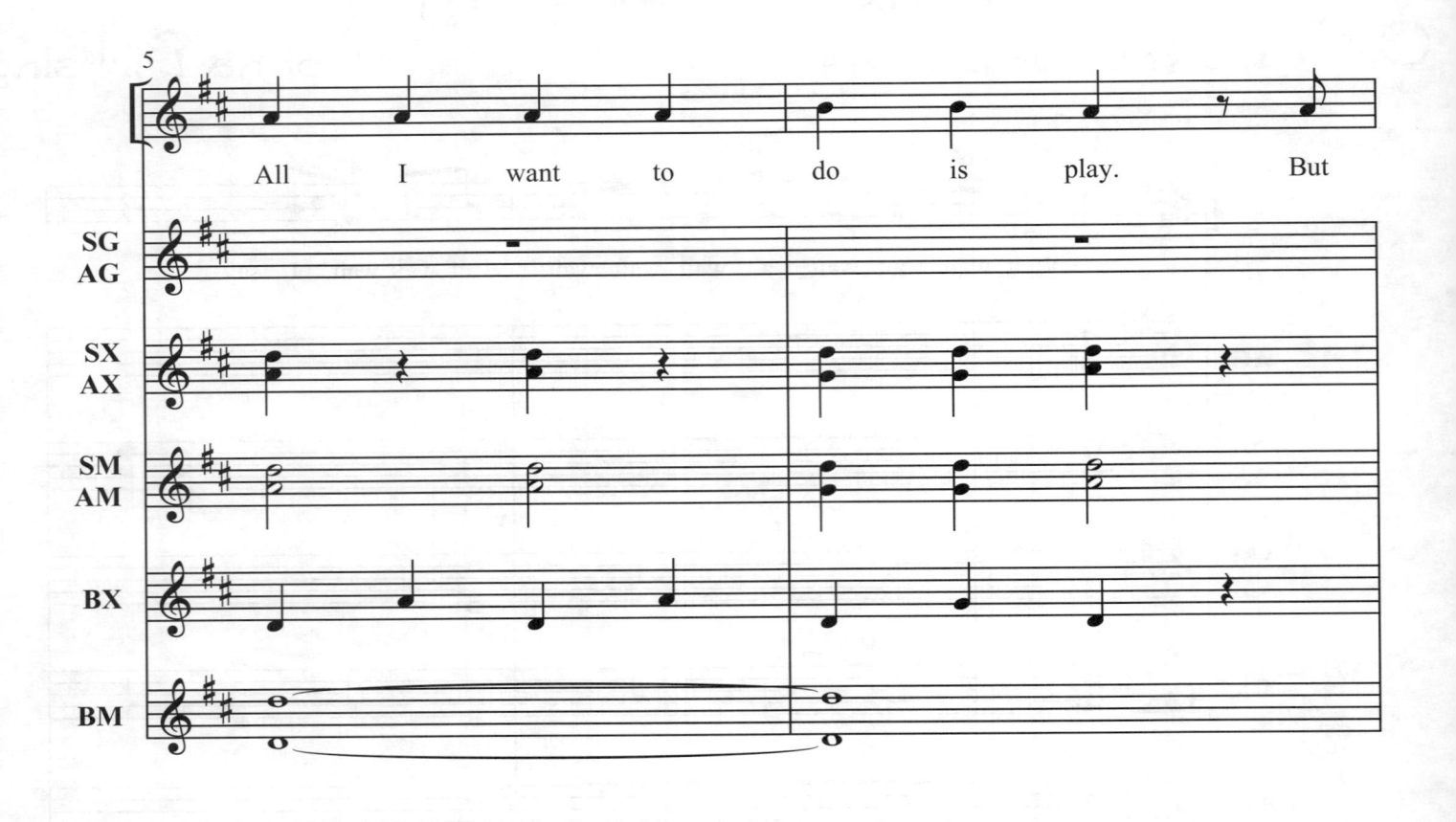

The Giant

Orff Accompaniment   **Donna Dirksing**

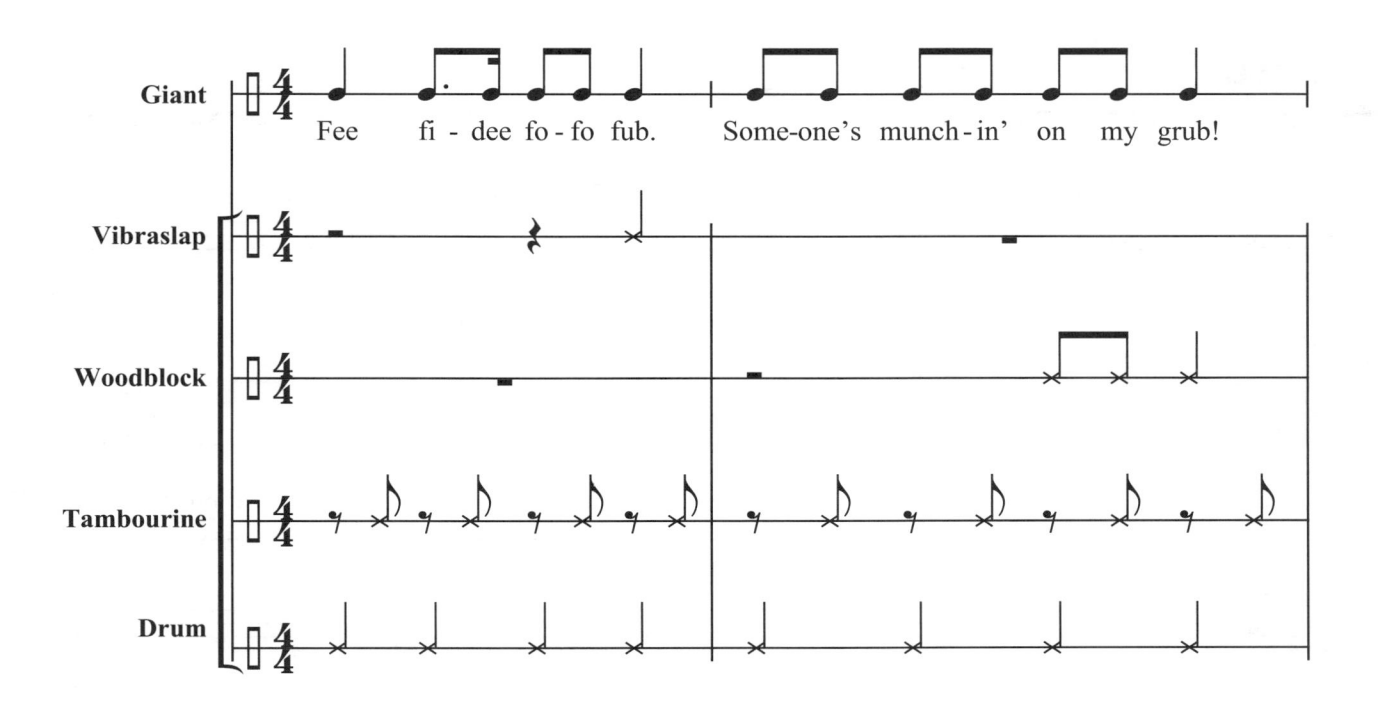

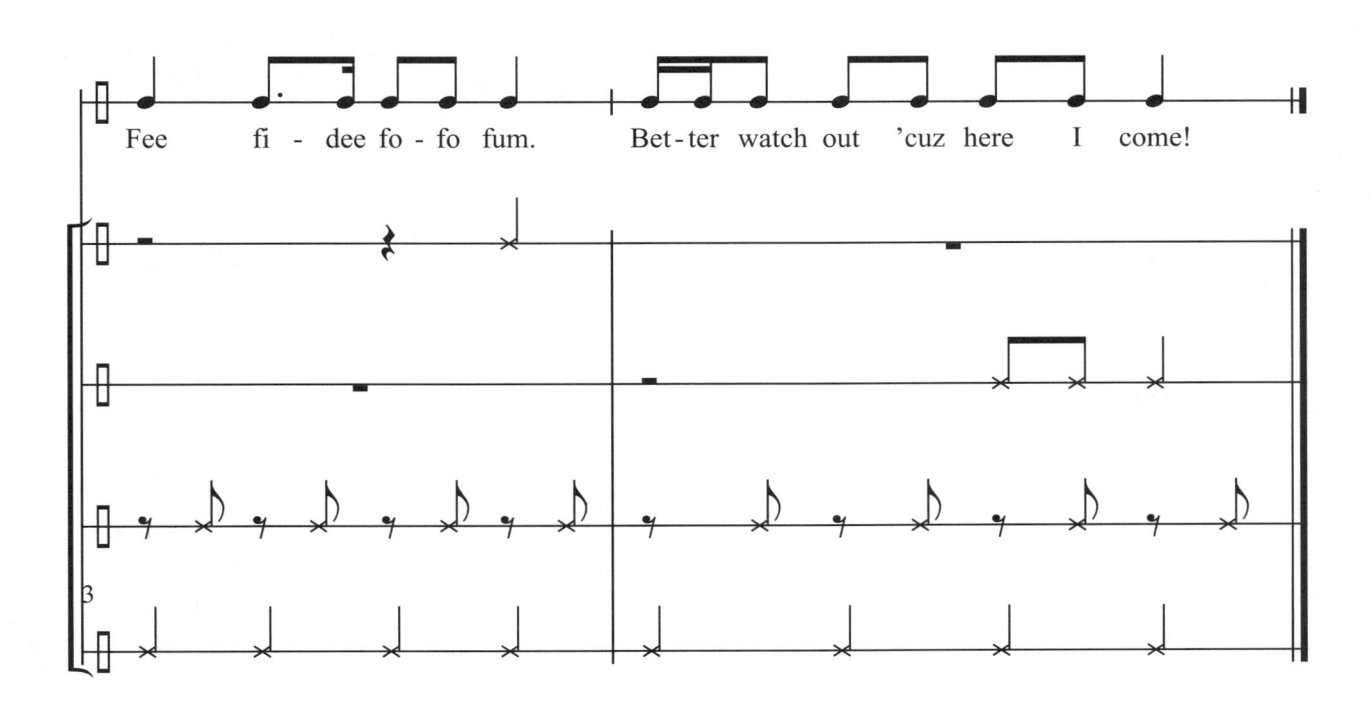

Giant: Fee fi - dee fo - fo fub. Some-one's munch-in' on my grub!

Fee fi - dee fo - fo fum. Bet-ter watch out 'cuz here I come!

Goldilocks and the Three Bears

One warm and sunny day Goldilocks was playing in the forest.

♪ Sing *Yonder Come Day*

Swing It!

Yon-der come day, Day is a-break-in',— Yon-der come day,
Oh, my— soul.— Yon-der come day, Day is a-break-in',—
Sun is a-ris-in'— in my soul.— Oh, well-a in my soul.— *Yeah!*

Goldilocks realized that she was lost and began to look for her way home. She followed a path and came upon a house. Goldilocks knocked on the door and waited but nobody answered.

34   From *Traditional Tales to Sing and Tell*, by Donna Dirksing. Permission to reproduce is granted for single-classroom use.

Being the curious mind that she was, Goldilocks opened the door and took a look inside. She spied three bowls sitting on the table. The bowls were filled with homemade chocolate pudding!

Goldilocks was very hungry from playing in the forest all day and she absolutely loved homemade pudding. She decided to have a little taste of the pudding in the great big bowl. It was too hot!

Too hot!

So she tried a taste of the pudding in the medium-sized bowl. It was too cold!

Too cold!

She tasted the pudding in the teeny tiny bowl and it was just right. Before she knew it, Goldilocks had eaten the pudding all up!

Naughty Goldilocks!

From *Traditional Tales to Sing and Tell*, by Donna Dirksing. Permission to reproduce is granted for single-classroom use.

Her belly was full and now Goldilocks wanted to rest for a little bit. She climbed upon a great big chair but it was too hard.

Too hard!

She climbed into a medium-sized chair but it was too soft.

Too soft!

Goldilocks sat upon a teeny tiny chair but she broke the chair to bits!

Naughty Goldilocks!

Goldilocks was still so tired that she didn't even clean up the mess. She needed to take a nap and she saw that there were three beds in the next room.

Goldilocks took one look at the great big bed and knew that it would be too hard.

Too hard!

She took one look at the medium-sized bed and knew that it would be too soft.

Too soft!

Goldilocks smiled as she lay upon the teeny tiny bed. It was just right! Soon she fell fast asleep.

Shh!

Goldilocks didn't hear the three bears as they returned home from their walk. As they looked around their house the bears saw that something was very different with their bowls of pudding.

"Somebody tasted my pudding!" said the Papa Bear.
"Somebody tasted my pudding!" said the Mama Bear.
"Somebody tasted my pudding and they tasted it all up!" said the Baby Bear.

♪ Sing *Somebody Tasted Your Pudding*

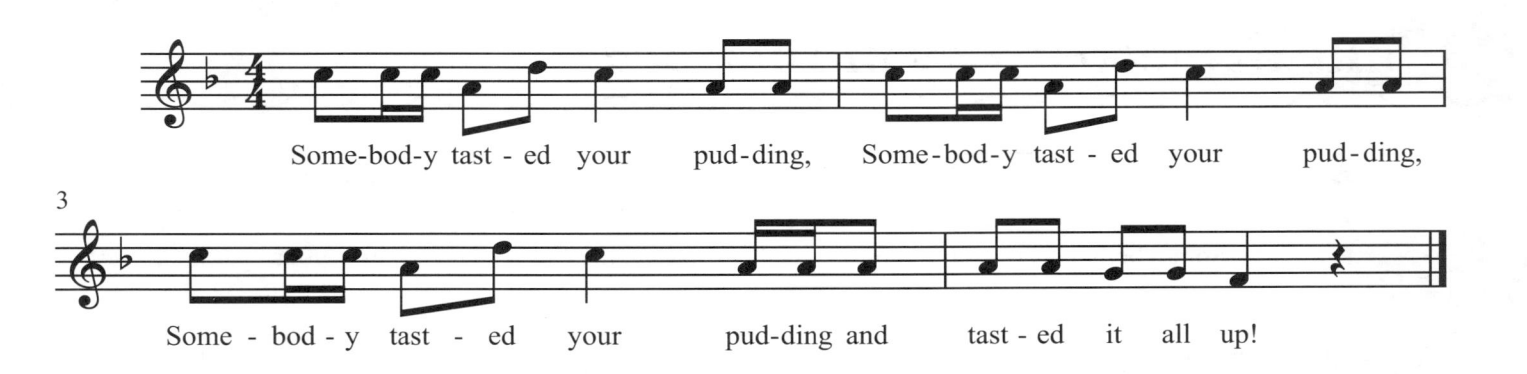

Some-bod-y tast-ed your pud-ding, Some-bod-y tast-ed your pud-ding,
Some-bod-y tast-ed your pud-ding and tast-ed it all up!

From *Traditional Tales to Sing and Tell*, by Donna Dirksing. Permission to reproduce is granted for single-classroom use.

Next the bears saw that something was very different with their three chairs.

"Somebody sat in my chair!" said the Papa Bear
"Somebody sat in my chair!" said the Mama Bear
"Somebody sat in my chair and they sat the bottom out!"
said the Baby Bear.

🎵 Sing *Somebody Sat in Your Chair*

Some-bod-y sat in your chair, Some-bod-y sat in your chair, Some-bod-y sat in your chair and sat the bot-tom out!

The three bears walked into their bedroom and saw something very different with their three beds. They had company!

"Somebody lay on my bed!" said the Papa Bear.
"Somebody lay on my bed!" said the Mama Bear.
"Somebody lay on my bed and she's still here!"
said the Baby Bear.

🎵 Sing *Somebody Lay in Your Bed*

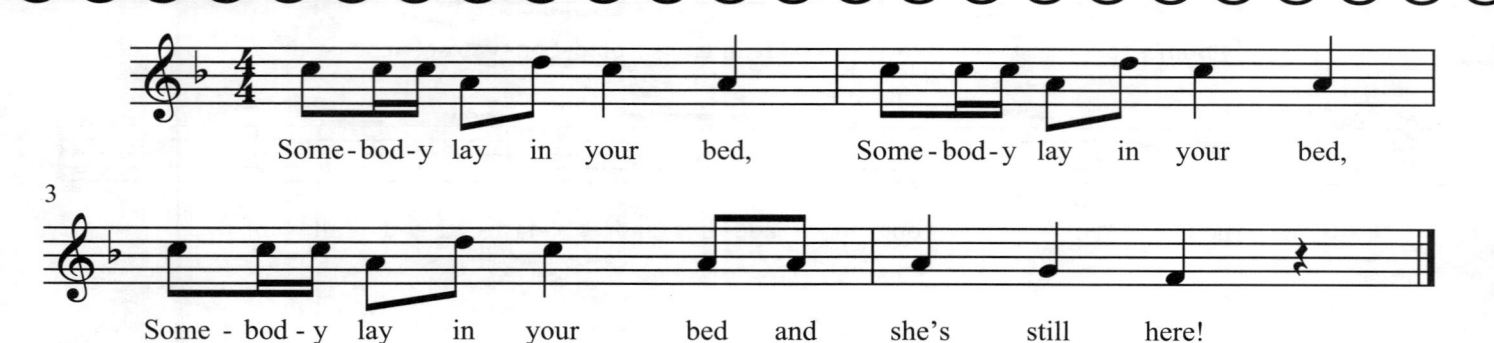

Some-bod-y lay in your bed, Some-bod-y lay in your bed, Some-bod-y lay in your bed and she's still here!

Goldilocks suddenly woke up from a deep nap and saw three bears smiling at her. At first she was nervous and wanted to run away. But Goldilocks courageously thanked the bears for their kindness.

She complimented the delicious homemade chocolate pudding and she apologized for breaking the teeny tiny chair and she promised to fix it. But the three bears kept smiling at the young girl. They were simply excited to meet a new friend. So Goldilocks and the bears went outside to play in the forest and enjoy the rest of the warm and sunny day.

🎵 Sing *Yonder Come Day*

Swing It!

Yon-der come day, Day is a-break-in',⎯ Yon-der come day,

Oh, my⎯ soul.⎯ Yon-der come day, Day is a-break-in',⎯

Sun is a-ris-in'⎯ in my soul.⎯ Oh, well-a in my soul.⎯ *Yeah!*

From *Traditional Tales to Sing and Tell*, by Donna Dirksing. Permission to reproduce is granted for single-classroom use.

Yonder Come Day

Yonder come day, day is a-breakin'

Yonder come day, oh my soul.

Yonder come day, day is a-breakin'

Sun is a-risin' in my soul! (Oh, well-a...)

From *Traditional Tales to Sing and Tell*, by Donna Dirksing. Permission to reproduce is granted for single-classroom use.

Somebody...

Somebody tasted your pudding,

Somebody tasted your pudding,

Somebody tasted your pudding,

And tasted it all up!

Somebody sat in your chair,

Somebody sat in your chair,

Somebody sat in your chair,

And sat the bottom out!

Somebody lay in your bed,

Somebody lay in your bed,

Somebody lay in your bed,

And she's still here!

From *Traditional Tales to Sing and Tell*, by Donna Dirksing. Permission to reproduce is granted for single-classroom use.

Yonder Come Day

Piano

Traditional
Arr. by Donna Dirksing

Lyrics:

Yon-der come day, Day is a-break-in', Yon-der come day, Oh, my soul. Yon-der come day, Day is a-break-in', Sun is a-ris-in' in my soul. Oh, well-a in my soul. *Yeah!*

42

Somebody...

Piano

Donna Dirksing

Some - bod - y tast - ed your pud - ding,
Some - bod - y sat in your chair,
Some - bod - y lay in your bed,

Some - bod - y tast - ed your pud - ding,
Some - bod - y sat in your chair,
Some - bod - y lay in your bed,

Some - bod - y tast - ed your pud - ding and tast - ed it all up!
Some - bod - y sat in your chair and sat the bot - tom out!
Some - bod - y lay in your bed and she's still here!

43

Yonder Come Day

Orff Accompaniment

Traditional
Arr. by Donna Dirksing

Yon-der come day, Day is a-break-in',

Yon-der come day, Oh, my soul.

5
Yon-der come day,
Day is a-break-in',
Sun is a-ris-in'
SG
AG
SX
AX
BX
8
1
2
in my soul. Oh, well a
in my soul.
Yeah!

Somebody...

Orff Accompaniment — Donna Dirksing

Some-bod-y tast-ed your pud-ding, Some-bod-y tast-ed your pud-ding,
Some-bod-y sat in your chair, Some-bod-y sat in your chair,
Some-bod-y lay in your bed, Some-bod-y lay in your bed,

Some-bod-y tast-ed your pud-ding and tast-ed it all up!
Some-bod-y sat in your chair, and sat the bot-tom out!
Some-bod-y lay in your bed, and she's still here!

46

The Diggity Drummer of DawgTown

The residents of DawgTown had a problem: Too many cats! It all started several years ago when someone brought some cats to town. "They will be so much fun to chase! Imagine the great times that we will have!" the awgTownie told his neighbors.

♪ Sing Cats

Swing It! (♫ = ♩♪)

We are the cats. And that is that. The dogs bark and fuss—'cuz they don't want us—to hang a-round in their town.— What can we say? We play all day. We play lots of tricks.— We love to hide their sticks.— That's why they don't want us a-round.—

From Traditional Tales to Sing and Tell, by Donna Dirksing. Permission to reproduce is granted for single-classroom use.

But the cats multiplied and multiplied until there were way too many to chase. Soon there were way too many to handle. Everyone knew that something needed to be done about all the cats in DawgTown.

🎵 Sing *Cats*

The mayor of DawgTown called a town meeting. "The cat problem in DawgTown is out of control and we must take action. I call upon the Diggity Drummer of DawgTown. There isn't a cat in town that can resist the rhythm of his drum. He will lead the cats out of our town."

The Diggity Drummer of DawgTown immediately grabbed his drum and softly began to play.

Cats everywhere stopped in their tracks, smitten by the rhythm of the drum.

From *Traditional Tales to Sing and Tell*, by Donna Dirksing. Permission to reproduce is granted for single-classroom use.

Sing *The Dawg Song*

Swing It!

I'm the dig-gi-est dawg a-round. I'm the dig-gi-est drum-mer of Dawg-Town. Lis-ten to the beat. Hear my sound. You should see the cats when I'm a-round. Cats can't han-dle my cra-zy beat. They wig-gle and they jig-gle and they stomp their feet. Their bod-ies start a-groov-in' to my rhy-thm sweet. *Whew!* Turn down the heat! Cats can't han-dle my cra-zy beat. They wig-gle and they jig-gle and they stomp their feet. Their bod-ies start a-groov-in' to my rhy-thm sweet. *Sweet!*

The Diggity Drummer smiled and played a little louder and then even louder. Soon all the cats in DawgTown came running toward the sound of the drum.

Sing *The Dawg Song*

From *Traditional Tales to Sing and Tell*, by Donna Dirksing. Permission to reproduce is granted for single-classroom use.

The Diggity Drummer led the parade of cats out of DawgTown playing his drum the entire time.

🎵 Sing *The Cats 'n' the Dawg*

Swing It!

Cats: We are the cats. And that is that. The dogs bark and fuss 'cuz they don't want us to hang around in their town. What can we say? We play all day. We play

Dawg: I'm the dig-gi-est dawg around. I'm the dig-gi-est drum-mer of Dawg-Town. Lis-ten to the beat. Hear my sound. You should see the cats when I'm a-round. Cats can't han-dle my cra-zy beat. They wig-gle and they jig-gle and they stomp their feet. Their

50   From *Traditional Tales to Sing and Tell*, by Donna Dirksing. Permission to reproduce is granted for single-classroom use.

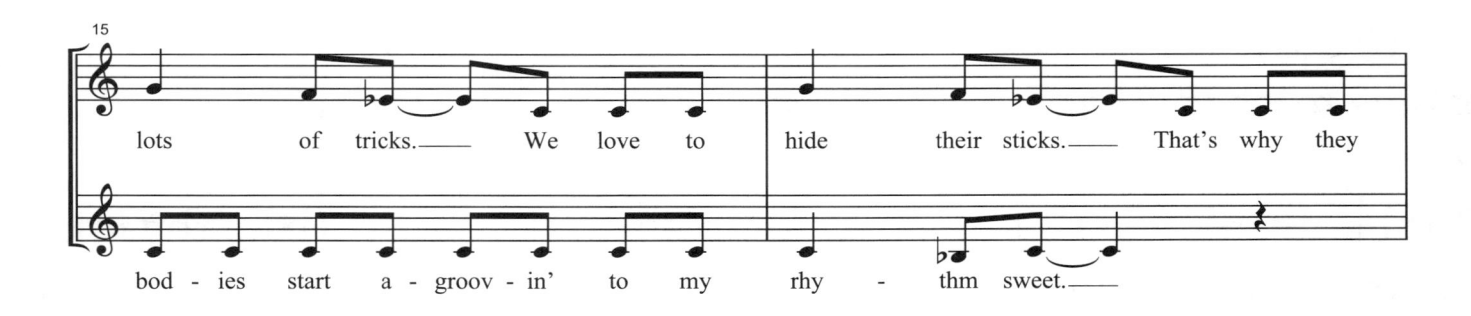

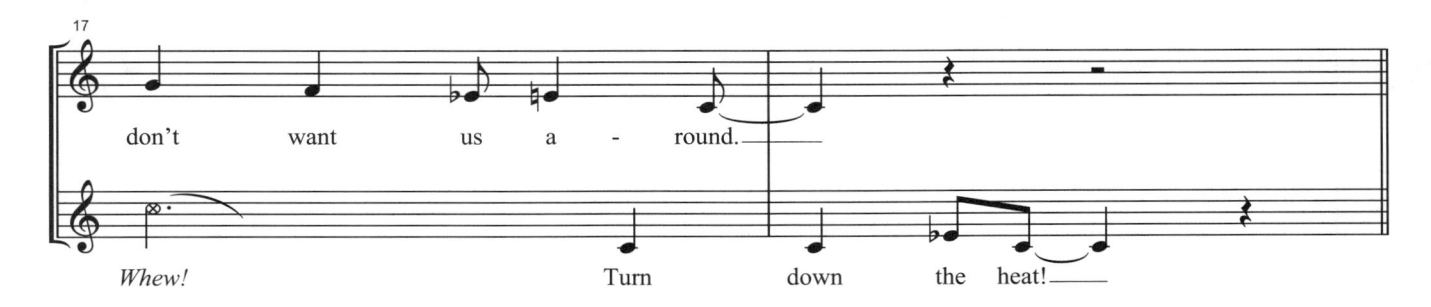

15 lots of tricks. We love to hide their sticks. That's why they
bod-ies start a-groov-in' to my rhy-thm sweet.

17 don't want us a-round.
Whew! Turn down the heat!

19 *Cats Scat, "Meow...Meow..." intermittently. Be sure to use different pitches and rhythms.*
Cats can't han-dle my cra-zy beat. They wig-gle and they jig-gle and they

22 stomp their feet. Their bod-ies start a groov-in' to the —

24
Sweet!
rhy-thm sweet.
Sweet!

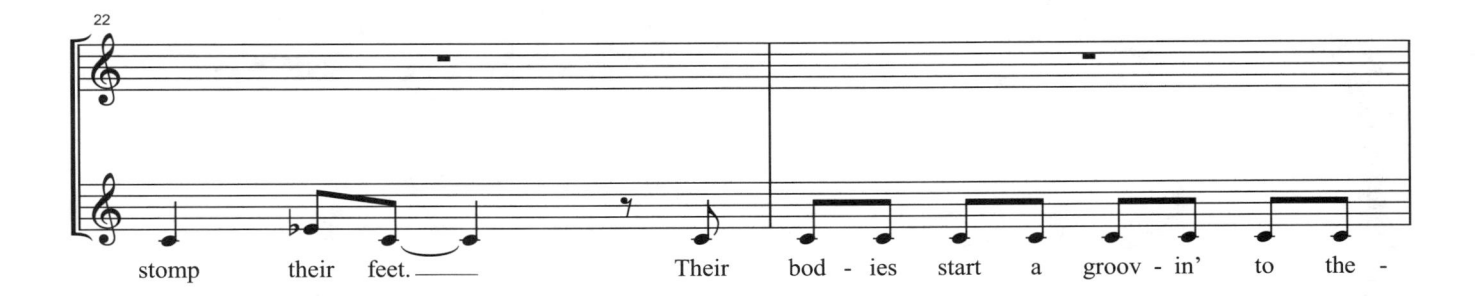

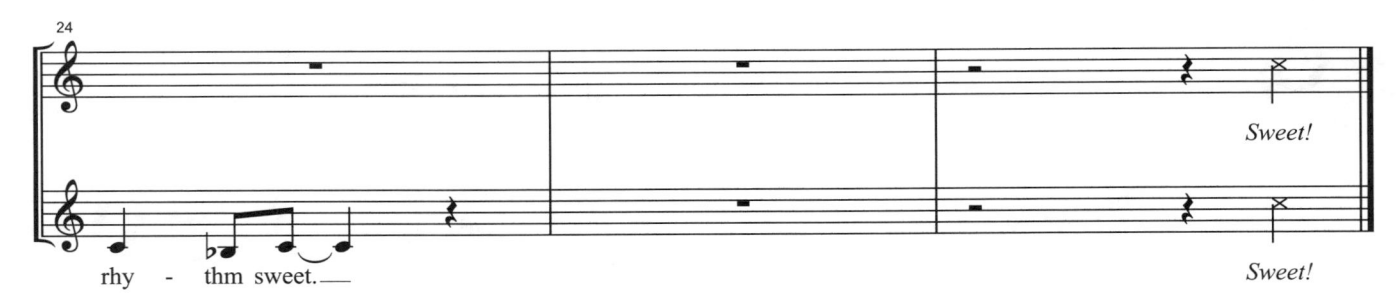

The cats eagerly followed the enchanting rhythms through the woods, over the hills, and down in the valleys.

🎵 Sing *The Cats 'n' the Dawg*

From *Traditional Tales to Sing and Tell*, by Donna Dirksing. Permission to reproduce is granted for single-classroom use.

The Diggity Drummer did not stop playing even when he and his cat parade reached a barnyard that was far from DawgTown.

This barnyard had a bit of a mice problem and over the years the mice had multiplied a hundred times a hundred times. The Diggity Drummer of DawgTown knew that the mice in this barnyard would definitely keep the cats busy.

He began to play his drum softer and softer until the cats could no longer hear his captivating rhythms and then he left for good.

The cats quickly turned their attention to chasing the hundreds of thousands of mice. And that is what they are still doing today.

Cats

We are the cats.

And that is that.

The dogs bark and fuss 'cuz they don't want us

To hang around in their town.

What can we say?

We play all day.

We play lots of tricks. We love to hide their sticks.

That's why they don't want us around.

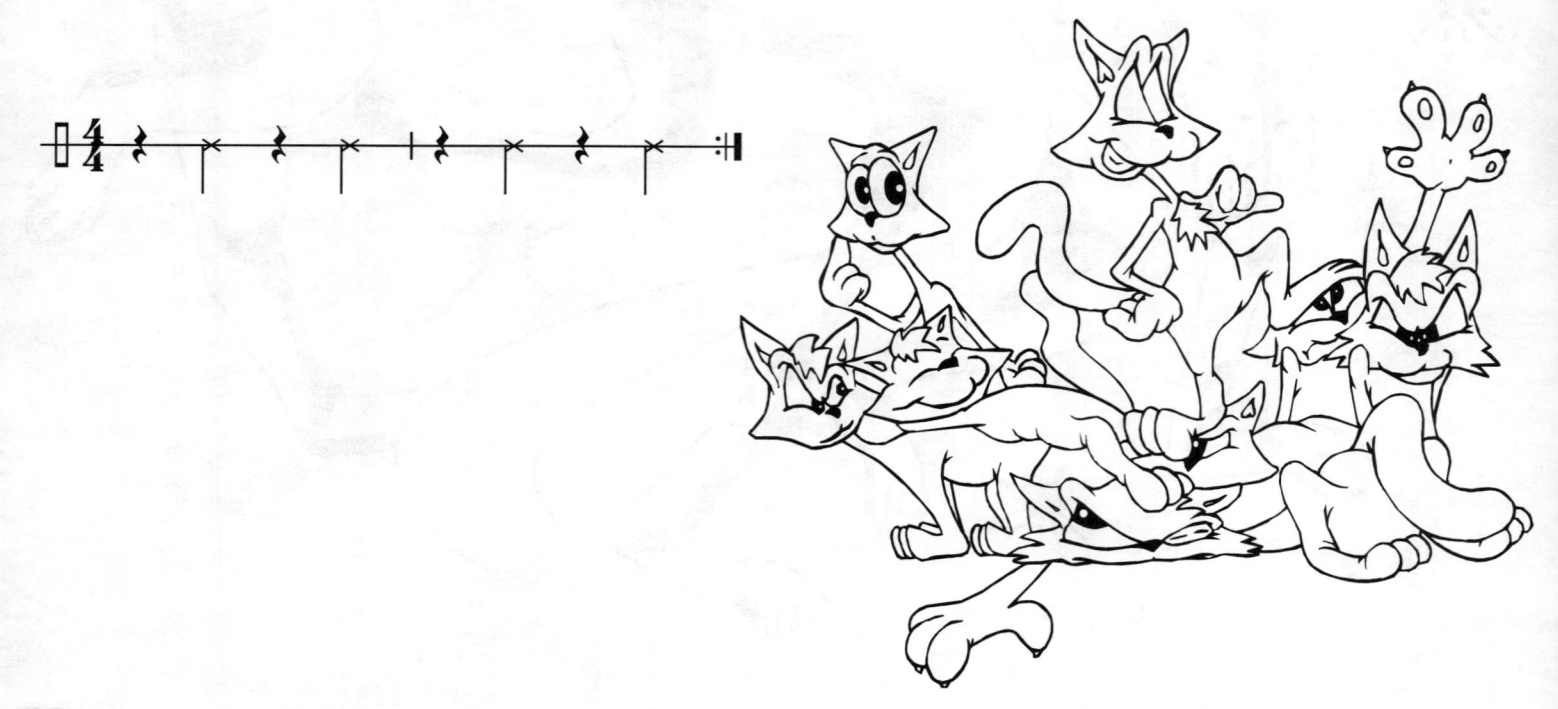

From *Traditional Tales to Sing and Tell*, by Donna Dirksing. Permission to reproduce is granted for single-classroom use.

The Dawg Song

I'm the diggiest dawg around.

I'm the diggiest drummer of DawgTown.

Listen to the beat. Hear my sound.

You should see the cats when I'm around.

Cats can't handle my crazy beat.

They wiggle and they jiggle and they stomp their feet.

Their bodies start a-groovin' to my rhythm sweet.

Whew! Turn down the heat!

Cats can't handle my crazy beat.

They wiggle and they jiggle and they stomp their feet.

Their bodies start a-groovin' to my rhythm sweet.

Sweet!

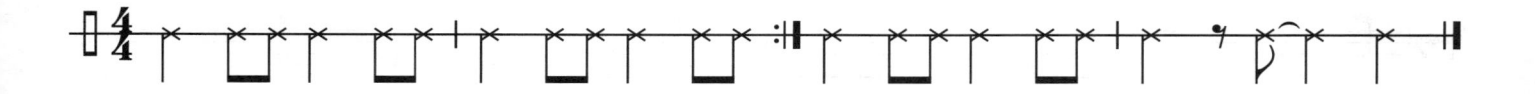

From *Traditional Tales to Sing and Tell*, by Donna Dirksing. Permission to reproduce is granted for single-classroom use.

The Cats 'n' the Dawg

Piano   Donna Dirksing

Swing It! (♫ = ♩♪)

Cats: We are the cats.

Dawg: I'm the dig-gi-est

And that is that. The dogs *(simile to m. 18)*

dawg a-round. I'm the dig-gi-est drum-mer of Dawg-Town. *(simile to m. 26)*

bark and fuss __ 'cuz they don't want us __ to hang a-round in their town. Lis-ten to the beat. Hear my sound. __ You should see the cats when

What can we say? We play all I'm a-round. __ Cats can't han-dle my cra-zy beat. __ They

day. We play wig-gle and they jig-gle and they stomp their feet. __ Their

15
lots of tricks. We love to hide their sticks. That's why they
bod-ies start a-groov-in' to my rhy-thm sweet.

17 *(snaps end)*
don't want us a-round.
Whew! Turn down the heat!

19 *Cats Scat, "Meow...Meow..." intermittently. Be sure to use different pitches and rhythms.*

Cats can't hand-le my cra-zy beat. They wig-gle and they jig-gle and they

58

stomp their feet. Their bod-ies start a groov-in' to the

rhy-thm sweet.

Sweet!

Sweet!

The Cats 'n' the Dawg

Orff Accompaniment   **Donna Dirksing**

bark and fuss ___ 'cuz they don't want us ___ to hang a-round in their town. ___

Lis-ten to the beat. Hear my sound. ___ You should see the cats when

___ What can we say? We play all

I'm a-round. ___ Cats can't han-dle my cra-zy beat. ___ They

day. We play

wig-gle and they jig-gle and they stomp their feet. ___ Their

61

15

lots of tricks. We love to hide their sticks. That's why they

bod-ies start a-groov-in' to my rhy-thm sweet.

17
(shaker ends)

don't want us a-round.

Whew! Turn down the heat!

19 *Cats Scat, "Meow...Meow..." intermittently. Be sure to use different pitches and rhythms.

Cats can't hand-le my cra-zy beat. They wig-gle and they jig-gle and they

62

stomp their feet. Their bod-ies start a groov-in' to the

rhy - thm sweet.

Sweet!

Sweet!

63